The Song of the Child

1st edition – December 2004
First Published – December 2004

Published by:

For further information contact **www.urpublications.com**

ISBN – 0-9736659-0-4

Printed by Crowes, 50 Hurricane Way, Norwich, UK

Dépôt légal: 4e trimestre 2004
Bibliothèque nationale du Québec

British Library Cataloguing-in-Publication Data
A catalogue record for this book is available from the British Library

Ur Publications and the Ur Publications logo
are trade marks of Ur Publications Ltd.

Book design by Mark Miller-Robshaw, Norwich, UK

Water colours scanned by Quadriscan Inc., Montréal, Qc, Canada
Cover: Wood crayons drawing by Sylvie Hétu

The Song of the Child

Sylvie Hétu

Canada-United Kingdom
www.urpublications.com

MISSION STATEMENT

Ur Publications wishes to bring to a wide readership, pioneering thinking at the leading-edge of evolving ideas within education, individual and social development, psychology and related fields – endeavouring to foster insight and creative impulses in these domains of human culture.

OUR UNDERTAKING

In accordance with social philosopher Rudolf Steiner's indications on the social question and the 'Three-fold Social Order' – in which human activities are arranged into three distinct, self-managed, and relatively autonomous spheres, viz. the cultural, the political, and the economic – Ur Publications guarantees to use a substantial proportion of its surplus to support cultural sphere activities, such as arts and education, according to associative economics principles.[1]

[1] For more information about associative economics, visit www.ae-institute.com

To the memory of my father,
Jean-Claude, who was always proud of me.

To my mother, Mona, a living example of
quiet, deep wisdom.

To my brother, Raymond, the expression of
a passionate free spirit.

To my sister, Diane, with whom I learned
the true meaning of playing in pure love.

To my brother of the heart, Dan,
who hears songs.

To Bibiane, a mother in spirit, who showed me a path
to perceive songs.

To my children – Étienne, Jean-Michel, and Joannie –
each of whom, in their unique ways,
has brought the Music of the Spheres into my life.

To Richard, my unique, with whom I sing.

ACKNOWLEDGEMENTS

The act of expressing ourselves, whether it be through teaching, talking, writing, or in any artistic way, requires a form of courage, or a kind of will. The publication of this book was made possible for me, first, because of the deep unconditional love of my family members to whom I have dedicated this book, as well as the love of my core friends – those who assist me to feel so deeply within every cell of my being that I am forever loved and trusted, no matter what the circumstances: Benedetta Costa, Paul Décarie, DeAnna Elliott, Mia Elmsäter, Maggy Faddoul, Denis Gossard, Pascale Graham, Annette James, Eric Longsworth, Kurt Mueller, Erica Nievwerhuis, Sylvie Pasquin, Kate Pigeon-Owen, Johanne Rochefort, Monique Van Gent, and Debra Zatelny.

Special thanks to Debra, Eric, and Sylvie, who, with great enthusiasm, said 'Publish!' after reading the original manuscript. Special thanks to Sylvie, too, for deciphering my handwriting. And very special thanks to Richard House, who has been an amazing midwife for the birth of my book (and for others to come), and for his greatly appreciated editorial skills.

Special thanks also to DeAnna Elliott, who shared the village tale with me.

Tremendous gratitude to Fiona Cooper, who believed in this project and gave it all her expertise in the publishing domain.

All my gratitude also to Geneviève Hogue, the woman who knows so much about administration and who is just so efficient and reliable, and under whose guidance Ur Publications is taking its first steps into the world.

Special thanks to Mark Miller-Robshaw, for his most appreciated logo and book designing skills. He always knew, within a few minutes, what my wishes were.

Many thanks to Geneviève Hogue (Ur Publications), Kate Pigeon-Owen (Childways Ltd), and Suzanne and Doug Reese (Compassionate Child Inc.) for being the first distributors of *The Song of the Child.*

Thanks to Vimala McClure, founder of the International Association of Infant Massage (I.A.I.M.), for her inspiration, for her vision, for her friendship. She has my profound admiration for her stance in making the world a better place to be for all children.

And special gratitude to Elaine N. Aron, Ph.D., author of the book *The Highly Sensitive Person*, which has inspired me so much, and finally led me to have a truly positive vision of my own puzzle – a quantum leap in hearing my own song.

Finally, I acknowledge, thank, and express gratitude to all my many, many friends and colleagues around the planet, and to all of you, holding this book in your hands, for your love of all children in the world.

CONTENTS

PART ONE

BEFORE HEARING THE SONG…

PART TWO

THE SONG…

The Song in minor

PREFACE

Every parent – all parents in every part of the world – do the best they can for their child. All of them. They do what they can from where they are in their own lives, in their heart, in their mind. They may sometimes have no idea what to do. You may think that some parents sometimes do awful things! – and that is right. But when awful things do happen, perhaps it is simply what parents are able to do at the time – for perhaps they possess nothing that would give them any clue as to what else might be done.

Every child who has been abandoned, neglected, abused, left alone, has suffered. And every parent whose behaviour has created any of these outcomes has suffered just as much.

I have simply written this book because, as a human community, it is my belief that we need to make steps toward greater consciousness of our own human nature. Every little step matters – not least in terms of the 'peace' for which we all yearn – whether it be in the world or in our own hearts.

This book presents a view from another, possibly new angle, and each road has different scenery to offer.

Sylvie Hétu
Eye, Suffolk, England
April 2003

AN IMPORTANT NOTE OF CAUTION

This book was written for ***adults*** alone. Please avoid using it with, or reading it to, children.

Thank you.

PRELUDE

Somewhere in a little village, well hidden in a forest on our planet, there is a community of people who have lived there from the beginning of time.

In that little village, when a baby is born the mother 'hears' a song – a song for that baby, for that baby who is born to life.

Other women in the village then learn this song, and sing it to the whole village.

Then the baby is introduced to all, and everyone in the village sings the song, that baby's song, to the baby.

Everyone in the village has her or his song. This song is unique to each, and is sung all through life.

When the person dies, the village sings that person's song.

Each of us has a song.

FOREWORD

by **Margot Sunderland**

This book is designed to empower adults to relate to children in ways which will enable the latter to thrive. In our technological society it is all too easy to lose touch with the potential wonders of a child's mind. It is all too easy to live exclusively in a left-brain world of facts, strategies, plans, and rules, and then find yourself unable to relate to children any more. In fact, in the UK the average child watches television for 21 hours a week, and spends only 38 minutes a week in meaningful conversation with parents (*British Medical Journal*, April 1999). Moreover, speaking with a child does not automatically mean connecting with them, connecting in the sense that the child feels profoundly met. At times, adults fail to relate well with a child because they have become detached from their own capacity for creative imagining, spontaneity, and the ability to live in the moment. This book therefore enters into the mind of a child as an inspirational wake-up call to equip adults to relate to children in ways which will enable them to flourish. Reading as a kind of modern fairy tale, it's a book all about connecting with children in new imagined ways so that they can feel deeply heard and seen.

When children are fortunate enough to be with an adult who can really connect with them, they will become co-travellers on the richest journey into sensorial reality and the world of the imagination. This book inspires the adult for such journeys, which, if repeated over time, will truly develop the child's social, emotional, and imaginal intelligence.

The voice of the child is beautifully portrayed in the book, and the reader will experience the child's deepest pain as well as their giddy heights of states of awe, wonder, and creativity. In this sense, the book will be an inspiration to parents, educators, teachers, psychologists, therapists, counsellors - in fact, anyone being with children.

Through her work in parent–infant massage – an innovative kind of baby massage which covers over 40 countries worldwide – Sylvie Hétu has been teaching parent–infant interaction all around the globe for many years, in all continents and with many and varied cultures and populations. This, coupled with her work as a Steiner (Waldorf) teacher and international lecturer, has given her exceptional insights into the child's world of spontaneity, imagination, and multi-sensorial perceptions of the world.

I will end with a passage from the book: 'We will watch the birth of a butterfly, opening with strength and courage its wrinkled wings to the gentle wind and the warm rays. You will tell me that maybe butterflies are flying flowers.' And so from being able to enrich the life of the child by meeting them fully in their world, the life of the adult is equally inspired.

Margot Sunderland
Director of Education & Training, Centre for Child Mental Health, London, UK;
UK Council for Psychotherapy (UKCP) Registered Integrative Child Psychotherapist

PART ONE

BEFORE HEARING THE SONG

Introduction from the child

You have big words that I do not understand yet. You classify everything, including me. Not only do you classify me, but you classify what I do. Not only do you classify it, but you analyse it. Then, you are able to evaluate me. You mark all sorts of things about me on your papers. You check all sorts of columns, squares, circles, and lines about me. Then you have all your numbers and ticked boxes about me, and it makes you happy. You think you now know me. I am in your mind and on your papers. Then you try to make me fit in some little squares or boxes that are in your computers or on your sheets, but which you've not checked. Some of you, indeed, have even nicer papers and machines where there are little squares about how my heart is feeling. That is good, and did leave me feeling a little more understood. Oh! I know, I know you work hard for me. I am most grateful. Oh! I know how pure is your intention with me. I am most grateful. If I decide to write to you today, it is to give you a break from your papers, your machines, and your measures.

My hope is that you will read with your heart, if that is something that can speak to you. Because as a child, I do not live in a world of marks and boxes. I still live in the world of images of the heart. That world is infinite and round. This is why it is so difficult to even put it into words.

My wish is that the words that I have chosen will bring you into that infinite round-heart-world of images.

One last thing. I know that some of you are able to measure things in my body and in my brain. You have special wires for that. That is quite magical for me, as some of the things you saw happened in inaccessible, secret places of my being. Some are revealed to you. I have recently been quite pleased to see the light in some of your eyes when you discovered that. The light of some of my secrets under certain conditions. Under re-created universes. Creating light in your adult universe. If you want to continue to discover some of my secrets in this way, you have my permission. Because of the light in your eyes. But please never forget that there will always be something of me that your computers will never see. Never. Only the eyes of your heart will.

Above all, remember that you will have more and more light in your eyes if you remember that within all my secrets is hidden a song. My song.

If you look for that song as an echo of your own song, and if you all sing me your songs, we will make a beautiful chorus together.

My universe is infinite, is unique, and it sings.

A wish

I wish that adults having this book in their hands will engage in an experience.

I wish for a willingness to be led to a conscious discovery of our own developing ability, faculty, to imagine... the wolf and the dragon... and the Knight... and the Queen... and the forest... and the All.

The never-ending discovery of the infinite possibilities of our living imagination is, I believe, a crucial key to truly meeting with the children in our care, to meet with all children – the ones we were, the ones around us now, the ones to come.

I wish that we would engage ourselves in an open and evolving way, allowing ourselves to be surprised, to be curious before the unknown mysteries, before the unanswered questions – to be intrigued, still, about our forever surprising human nature.

Hope

I believe that hope is a motor, a driving-force that lives within each of us, as a possible path to make our world a better place to be. I have many hopes myself!

I do hope that this book will help to contribute, in a refreshing and even novel way, to a lessening of the manifold crises and general malaise that surround education.

I am deeply aware that thousands of books have been written to foster our adult consciousness about children's development and needs. I am aware, too, of all those who, like me, hope for a better understanding, leading in turn to better courses of action. I am aware of the pure, positive intent which all those involved in education possess, and I am truly grateful for each and every contribution to children's well-being, in whatever form and from whatever source.

The modest 'note' of freshness that I hope might be appreciated by the readers of this book is intended as an inspiring eulogy for the noble cause of 'hearing' children in a broader sense, so that we can enjoy singing all together, and more often.

I 'heard' the whole of *The Song of the Child* myself over four days in a beautiful village named Eye in England, in the county of Suffolk. All I had to do was to trust, and to commit it to paper, out of hope.

Preparation for reading – experiencing and practising 'hearing'

I invite you to read *The Song of the Child* as if you were reading a fairy tale. Fairy tales are, as we would say in French, from *La Nuit des Temps* (or 'the night beyond all times'). From 'ever', from eternity, and with no age. Fairy tales encompass archetypal attributes of human beings that are, and belong to, all cultures, that are beyond culture. They seem to be out of linear time; and they have a wisdom in themselve's – which is why true admirers of fairy tales suggest that we refrain from changing them or removing parts that we don't like, as such tampering can interfere with the unfolding evolution of the tale in all its archetypal richness, or disrupt the transformative resolution of unconscious aspects of our human nature which, if enabled, can strengthen important human faculties.

It is true that when we read fairy tales, parts of them may be challenging to our conscious day-to-day mind. Most of us, living as we do in modern times, wish only to focus on positive feelings and positive values, hoping that only such agreeable qualities will be manifest in our individual experience and behaviour. This is indeed a noble goal. However, darkness lives in all of us, and I can say that, personally, I embrace the idea of trying to live with it with awareness – the idea of taming our darkness so that we can become its master. I also believe that this is one central role of traditional fairy tales – that is, to enable us to develop inner capacities and faculties that will help us to be lighter than our darkness, and that will lead us to transform those shadowy aspects. If one reads fairy tales over and over again, it can be observed that there is often a transformation of 'lower qualities' into higher, lighter ones, and an embracing of wisdom and courage in the process.

While reading *The Song of the Child,* the reader is invited to remain open to what could be called 'the archetypal' in each and every child. The 'child' referred to in this book has no specific age, and can be of any age. 'Images' can and will no doubt be born within each reader – images of any child, of any age; a known one or an imagined one. All is possible.... For one image, it could be a baby, for another one a child, or a teenager. For each image it can be of any and all ages. It can be a memory of you as a child, or even as an adult which still has the child aspect within, as we can all experience at times.

Each motif – and there is one on each page of *The Song* – can hologramically reveal all in everything, for each and every reader. These multiple motifs are not intended to be read or understood as strict 'causes' of various expressions of the inner life of a child. Rather, they are simply *possible* manifestations. They are drawn from what might be called 'an intuition married with knowledge' about children, gained through my many years of experience as a teacher, educator, and mother, as well as the large number of books I have read in the course of my studies, and the many lectures and classes I have attended. They may well also be born of some of my own will in overcoming personal-biographical challenges. If they speak to you, so be it. And if they do not speak to you – again, so be it. They are not intended to be used either as applicable 'solutions' or recipes for particular situations. Their real intent, again, is to inspire adults to enter into an inner imaginative movement or fluidity, so that the uniqueness of each child can start to be perceived and heard, in pure openness. And following on from this, perhaps new imaginative ways of reaching children will be experienced by caring adults, resulting in each and every child opening to becoming what their destiny calls forth.

Words on imagination

Imagination is a human faculty. It is the faculty of being able to create inner images. It develops through our various growth stages, hopefully to become, in our adult lives, a faculty we can consciously use to find creative ways of meeting life challenges, to create 'solutions', to invent, to practise artistic expression, to give birth to projects, and to develop flexible ways of sharing at all levels with other human fellows.

Reaching others requires from us the imaginative faculties to create a bridge to being understood, since each of us is unique and 'hears' or 'sees' in a unique way. 'I' have to use imagination to find a way to reach 'you', as 'you' are unique and different from 'her' or 'him', with whom I will also have to use my imagination to feel understood. Imagination can thus work in tandem with perception skills, serving inspiration and intuition that will lead to the best action-attitude-words in a given situation or encounter.

Children's imagination develops gradually and, if well protected and allowed to unfold at its natural pace, can be observed to be very pure, very one with itself and with the child him- or herself up to the age of seven. I am sure that most readers will remember themselves not 'believing' in fairies or Father Christmas or monsters, but being sure they exist!

Imagination is not yet separated from 'reality' for young children. Making the difference between the 'real' and the imagined comes slowly, and reaches a tipping-point around the age of nine years of age, where, expressed as an image, the child starts to feel the difference between the gods and human beings, between heaven and earth, between lightness and heaviness, between good and bad, between black and white. Before that age, when the child's consciousness is still normally dreamy, not sharp, not yet awoken, not divided like that of adults, it is truly impossible for the child to grasp how adults rationally think. They may *appear* to understand what we tell them, what we explain to them; they may somehow understand the words in their inner self and mind, but they haven't yet reached the adult way of thinking. Deeply, they do not understand.

We adults use our imagination if we wish to. Children *are* imagination. This is why, for a young child, a wood-stick is a magic wand, becomes the magic wand for the purpose of her or his momentary activity. The same wood-stick can later be a rocket, a sword, a mobile phone, or a boat.

This wonderful process should be respected, encouraged, promoted, and, most of all, protected, for it is the basis, the foundation stone for a very important aspect of their future 'intelligence' that will enable them, as adults, to meet the world with the Goethean notion of an imaginative eye, an eye that sees beyond. This in turn may foster the potential to contribute to the world's evolution with conscious imagination.

At first, for the child, imagination is mainly awoken by the immediate world surrounding him. All simple objects can become all and everything serving his activities. Objects themselves will awaken the imaginative process. Then, later on, inner images will start to be born within the child, and will find expression through the child's activities where she will seek the objects serving her imagination, or where she will 'talk out loud' her imaginary world. 'Make believe' in its purest form....

Parents often worry if their child will ever grow out of his imaginary friends, or whether he will 'understand' that the monster is not 'real'.... They will do so naturally, as their first teeth start to fall out around the age of six. We grow in a visible way, physically, and we also grow in an invisible way, in our heart, soul, and mind.

What an effort it requires from us adults to 'remember' how a child thinks.... What an effort it requires from us to reach their world. It needs practice, and it needs from us sound, renewed knowledge of how we develop as human beings. It needs us to push away the idea that a child is a small adult. A child is a developing human being. The seed of a plant contains within it the whole potential of the plant, but is not yet a plant. Under proper balanced conditions, the plant will develop. But we cannot pull the leaves out of the stem, the fruit out of the flower. We provide and protect, so that the plant can develop.

On a very subtle level, if we develop adult rational thinking within a child who still lives in imagination in its pure, undivided expression, we pull him prematurely into a world that is not yet his to visit. We also remove from him the possibility of living and discovering and experiencing, in an undisturbed way, each natural stage of its development.

Can we leave children to be children? Can we leave them in their fantastic, positive imagination without giving them everything 'thought out' in advance for them? Can we allow them the space to re-create the world? Can we enjoy a rainbow in its whole magic, with treasure at its end, instead of explaining to them the decomposition of light through water, without speaking about spectra or about Newton? Can we let them *experience* the rainbow instead of explaining it to them? Can we let them imagine the rainbow living within their whole being? Can we allow them to experience pure awe?

In awe, if their own capacity to marvel is kept intact, in time they will reach their teen years, where they will be able to be in true wonder at the thought and explanations of the light spectrum.

Let us put on our magic boots to walk through the rainbow, to find what treasure it hides for us....

More on 'the note of caution'

At the beginning of this book there is a 'note of caution', emphasizing that this book should not be read by children, but only by adults. Although *The Song* may appear to be recounting a child speaking, and may appear to have been written with words easily understandable by children, this is not the case.

Rather, the words of *The Song* are expressions of possible inner soul moods experienced by children at unconscious levels. After many observations and much studying and learning, I profoundly believe that adults should stay away from making the child aware of what is deeply happening within her, as this type of awareness needs further development and adult maturity in order to be dealt with. In stating this, I am aware that I may create waves of opposition, as there has been much emphasis placed on educating children to be able to express their emotions. We speak a lot about 'emotional literacy'. I do agree with the goal, but I also wish for a rethinking of some of the ways in which we want to achieve this goal for the good of children and society. I will offer some explanations of my thinking, inviting the reader first to contemplate these other possibilities and, at least, to consider them. You could then refer to the 'Inspiring readings' section at the end of the book if you wish to pursue further avenues.

Here is a simple life example. A child has to welcome a new brother or sister. Nobody, no parent, can really predict the child's reactions, no matter how well loved and prepared he is. The child may experience a whole range of emotions of all colours. Some will bring reactions that may be a considerable distance from what the parents may have wished. There will be readjustment, created by the new situation. Every new life situation brings an imbalance, an upsetting of a previously existing equilibrium, and then the discovery of a new balance. This is a normal process!

So our child, yes, may be what we adults call 'jealous'. The child doesn't yet know about jealousy – rather, we could say the child *is* jealousy, and has a variety of unique, personal ways to live that jealousy. 'Talking' to the child about it is, in my opinion, very risky. The ability to talk about emotions requires enormous detachment, and enters a world of muddy waters that we, as adults, are still trying to negotiate. The child is whole, and feels much more than 'thinks'; and putting words on to these 'whole' feelings brings the child into detached, rational thinking that is an adult characteristic.

Our own wholeness, which includes compassion, attachment, empathy, and deep understanding, is what the child first has to feel from us. As adults, we are the ones who need to adjust to *their* universe, not the other way around, as they have not developed the capacities to inhabit our universe. They are, after all, children.

Our actions should be attuned to the child's stage of development, rather than imposing our own desired developmental goals, and this in turn requires every effort of imagination, as I have already described. Our attitudes and actions, our own feelings, tone of voice, body language, and touch will be what the child will answer to best; and not our analysing and interpretations of their emotions, and our attempts to teach them how to express them. I believe there to be too much classification and analysing of the emotional world, characteristic as it is of a very adult, scientific, matter-based world. I am not saying that the adult analytic brain is somehow wrong; I am merely saying that the detached, objective identification and naming of emotional states is far away from what a child needs in order to grow, to become strong and develop control over herself.

I believe that it narrows human potential if we do not embrace the fact that we are still substantially a *mystery* both for ourselves and also to others. I think that instead of bringing the child to a full experience of herself, it actually cuts her off from her wholeness, bringing her into premature objectivity when subjectivity should reign. The child, even if she would hear or learn to say 'It's hard for me to have a new baby in the house', would still be whole and suffering. Even if he were to hear 'Papa and mama still love you', the child needs to feel it, experience it, before anything else. And – not easy to embrace – the child needs to feel this love even, and perhaps even more, during the adjustment period.

Don't we, even as adults, need to feel love, when we feel all messed up, or when we mess up a situation? Don't we even feel that we want others to have deep compassion FOR and understanding of our wrong behaviour? This is one of the greatest paradoxes in life, and it certainly offers food for thought in the sphere of child raising. I certainly do not pretend to have all the answers, as paradoxes are paradoxes, and the path of human development is surely a path which still has many roads to be explored.

Here are some unresolved questions:

'What does a child really feel when you say: "I love you but I do not accept your behaviour", if we understand that a child is whole?'

'How does a child feel when deeply feeling us focussing on his behaviour, no matter whether it is good or bad, rather than on the core of his being, rather than on his song?'

'How do we then "raise" children to be social beings, as society and culture do encompass acceptable and unacceptable "behaviours"?'

'What do we do when a child kicks or bites, and hurts another child?'

So many questions....

The beginning of my own answers always goes back to the view of the child as a whole being, instead of focussing on the behaviour alone. We are not to be 'trained' as animals; we are to be raised to our highest potential, trusted that we can become a human being of unique beauty. My continuing efforts on the ongoing path of dealing with these paradoxes and questions entail that we ourselves strive to be what we feel a noble human being should be, and fully to live those strivings in the presence of children. I think that children – and we ourselves – would gain immeasurably if we could simply model for them sensitive and imaginative human qualities worthy of being imitated, rather than conveying an intellectual apprehension of the world that tends to constrain their experience.

Knowledge is vast and resides everywhere, and is made all the more easy to access with the new information technologies. Development is more subtle; and if we, as adults, continue to see ourselves as developing individuals, the very fact that we seek to develop will inspire children. It is the fact that we encounter life with 'an imaginative eye', as previously described, that will help provide children with the openness to finding solutions to their own challenges.

We do not pretend to understand everything, and we don't have quick answers to every situation, behaviour, and experience that our children encounter. I would like us to consider together:

allowing space for not knowing, leaving space for hope, for curiosity, for secrets and personal intimacy, for shadow and the unknown, to be left as they are;
allowing ourselves still to be surprised and in awe;
allowing room for what we cannot yet embrace, as our imagination may not have imagined yet.

In this sense, this book is a paradox in itself, even a contradiction, in the light of the previous discussion. This is the main reason why it should not be read to children, as I wish that they stay free of our 'identification of reasons', adult-based thinking, and reasoning. This is why I propose the book as an experience for adults to bring alive *their own* inner movement of interaction with children.

I propose the book, then, as a tool to stir imagination in adults in order to reach children's infinite mysterious universes. Imaginative expressions found in *The Song of the Child* could not be written by a child. They are already too 'conscious' for children, already too fixed, too explained; and this is where we swim in the paradox. Children, if surrounded by sensitive adults and surrounded by a safe environment, will experience, will *be* imagination, without us having to make them 'aware' of it. We can reach them through their imagination, through their games, their world, without having to describe it.

Imaginative expressions found in the book, if read to children, would bring them out of the experience, or would bring too much light to the eyes of their young souls. Let us give them time to prepare their eyes, time to develop.

Let us give them time to be children.

'Awareness' will surely come in time.

Thank you.

'Spiritual' knowledge of the child

In the course of my journey as a teacher, educator, trainer, and parent, I have met with many authors and schools of thought regarding child development and child education, and they have all touched me at various levels. This book would be incomplete without mentioning the work of the scientist-philosopher and educator Rudolf Steiner. Steiner lived from 1861 to 1925, and is the founder of Anthroposophy (meaning 'wisdom of man'), also referred to as the science of spirit. Through his painstaking work on investigating the deep nature of humanity as a whole and its evolution, including human beings in their individual grandeur, Steiner wrote more than 30 books and gave over 6,000 lectures around the world. He is for me an extraordinary genius. He gave humanity indications and knowledge about most spheres of human activity, ranging from agriculture, architecture, biology, medicine, and nutrition, to politics, social and personal development, education, and so on... – all of that, together with clearly articulated ways of developing that deep knowledge. From his indications, a range of inspired fields of research and activities has been 'born' on the planet, amongst which is the worldwide schooling movement called Waldorf education or Steiner education. This movement has been, and still is, of true inspiration to me.

A lot of resistance to Steiner education has been experienced for many reasons, perhaps the main one relating to the fact that there is what could be called 'spiritual' knowledge informing its foundations. This is absolutely true, and it has never been hidden or denied that Rudolf Steiner was a 'spiritual investigator'. Indeed, his ongoing investigation of humanity was thorough-goingly 'scientific', and he simply gave each and every one of us the possibility of developing this true knowledge through our own willingness to give it time, study, and interest, enabling anyone pursuing his indications to draw their own conclusions from their own investigations.

I believe that it is time for humankind collectively to embrace the very real possibility that there still exists a great mystery about just who we are, and that we would all benefit from deeply accepting that we are far away from having all the answers. Moreover, a collective humility and openness is surely required in order to create bridges between what we 'really know' and what remains in the realm of belief. I am no more than an investigator myself, but Rudolf Steiner's work has given me an extraordinary way into answering some of the mystery's secrets, to gain a bit of light that has in turn led me to further interesting questions. There is more in 'the invisible' than we can even imagine; and, again, this book is just one small exercise in bringing some inspiration for starting to imagine, and perhaps understand slightly better.

Gods, queens and kings, shepherds

It would disturb me very much if readers were to conclude from *The Song* that I am an advocate of 'let your child do whatever he wants to', for the good of his development and freedom of expression – for in no way is this the case. We again face a paradox here. Children need our adult guidance – strongly!.... But they also need 'freedom to become'. How to balance authority and freedom is surely one of the biggest questions facing all educators, whether parents or teachers.

Too much authority – authoritarianism – hinders the child's potential, bringing fear, shame, and low self-esteem, to name but a few of its negative effects. Neglect creates a void, which can lead to pure disengagement, or else to all kinds of 'Have you seen me?' gestures and actings-out. The excesses of a needs-driven education, together with the current fashion for relatively boundary-less 'freedom of expression', is now leading psychologists and educational researchers to rediscover forgotten perennial wisdoms, now proclaiming again that 'The child needs boundaries!'.... Parents and educators: reclaim your proper role! Matters are now turned upside-down, and children are now commanding their parents and teachers! Some authors even go so far as to state that we may have created a generation of superficially self-sufficient, self-centred young adults, insensitive to others' needs... not to mention young tyrants....

So where to go? This book is not about discipline; it is more about connecting with children in new imagined ways, so that they can be deeply heard, felt, seen, and allowed to become. Other writings are already available on positive discipline and social development for children, and others will surely appear.

For the moment, let me just share an 'image' that I received through my study of Steiner education, which I have found so inspiring as a basis for adult attitudes to child-rearing and education. It would feel amiss not to share it with the reader.

From 0 to 7 years old:

Adults are like 'Gods' for children. At this stage, children do not yet have the capacity for objectively evaluating what is right or wrong for them. They take in everything, and they imitate everything. Adults thus have a profound responsibility in having 'to be worthy of being imitated'. Adult actions, feelings, moods, words, and body language are themselves the 'teachers'. This is where there is a profound need for us to 'preach with our actions', to 'walk our talk'. Yes, it is a lot of work: everything, *everything* is 'believed' by the young child. Let us remember it.

From 7 to 14 years old:

Adults are seen as Queens and Kings by children. It is not the other way around.

The child is not the Queen or the King! Children deeply need the wise, strong, and reliably consistent authority of a good King, of a good Queen. They need to know from us where the kingdom lies, its beauty combined with its clear rules and identified territory. They also need to know that in the kingdom, there are other people living with the same rules. Having clearly identified Kings and Queens around them will enable children to develop sound inner security as well as appropriate social skills, so that, one day, they can venture out of the walls of the kingdom. Put on your crowns!

From 14 to 21 years old:

Ah! There is a world behind the great fortress of the beautiful kingdom! – I want to discover it! Our dear teenagers.... The Kings and Queens have to develop conscious trust and give conscious missions to their beloved 'subjects'.... Humility and trust, with a loving eye... qualities of the shepherd.... But... they are not Kings and Queens yet, these beautiful exploding adolescents!.... They need us to give them a chance to venture forth, yes. But they need us to understand discretely how frightened, lost, doubtful they may be, and they surely still need to know who the 'guardians' are; and they surely need the safety of the known kingdom, where the King and Queen still live, rule, and decide when to open the draw-bridge.

The two parts of the song

The first part, called 'The song in minor', develops expressions of what could be seen as shadowy, unregulated, troubled parts of the child. We all have these parts within us. Many philosophers, psychologists, psychiatrists, educators, therapists of all types, and parents have given them all sorts of names and classifications.

I could say that humanity as a whole is really trying very hard to grasp the idea of good and bad, light and shadow, yin and yang, evils, demons, and angels – whatever you may wish to call it. We are all still on a long journey with regard to understanding these matters.

The second part, called ' The song in major', shares expressions of what could be seen as the inner unconscious wisdom of each child, seeking an opening and guidance for its full manifestation.

Words about 'The Answer'

The third part of the book, called 'The Answer', wishes to bring images of possible 'soul attitudes' that adults might adopt, answering the child's archetypal expression to be found in *The Song.*

'The Answer' should, again, be read as planting seeds for the nurturing of a growing imaginative process, leading to multiple and varied forms of expression within each unique relationship between an adult and a child.

Hopefully, inspiration and intuition will come into play in all our approaches with children. Although the word 'intuition' in itself remains mysterious in all our attempts to describe it, there is something there that has guided many human beings toward an extraordinary blooming and birth in all spheres, from personal expression, social encounters, to pure creation in all spheres of life. Most of us have experiences where what we had decided upon, what we had thought objectively, what we had all organized, was blown away by a 'small voice' heard within. This can be so true in our ways of relating to children. Let us be surprised by whom they are trying to become, albeit perhaps in awkward ways; and let us be open to rethinking what we actually want to do to 'raise' them. Let us be open really to *hearing* all subtleties of tone – and let us be open to learning to sing with them rather than *to* them.

'The Answer' may sound naïve and simplistic to readers who have already dedicated their lives to the understanding of children. So be it.

I truly believe in the potential paradox of finding a path of light in a very simple way.

I truly believe that we have forgotten to embrace what is a profound simplicity, to encounter the infinite mystery of our human development.

I invite you to breathe into the imaginative simplicity that is 'The Answer', and I am grateful for your efforts to do so, and to welcome it into your own soul.

Positive naïveté

I HONOURING A TONE

For all those years of my life, up to the dawn of my 50th birthday, I have been struggling with an aspect of my own song that I have always called 'immature naïveté.' Now I have changed my mind about it, instead calling it *positive* naïveté, as this trait, I now realise, served and serves me, and will continue to serve me, in many and diverse ways! The two main features I wish to highlight here are the following: first, it leads people around me to smile and laugh; and second, it helps me to stay in tune with a tone that young children themselves naturally possess.

Up to now, only my close friends were given the opportunity to hear about some personal stories related to that trait. For the purpose of this book, however, and *The Song's* intent of encouraging readers to start practising imaginative fluidity in their own approach to caring for children, I will share two stories with you, 'The white lines' and 'The magic wand'.

II THE WHITE LINES

In my early twenties, I was studying education at the University of Montreal in Canada. One day, at lunch-time, I went walking with another student. It was a beautiful day, a clear blue sky with no clouds. As usual, I looked up to the sky. There it was, a long beautiful white line, created by the passage of an air plane. How nice!

It happened that I spontaneously started to talk to my student colleague: 'Isn't it nice that some pilots choose to put this special stuff in their plane so that beautiful white lines are created to decorate the sky? Plus, have you noticed that they often choose to do it when the sun is about to set so that the lines become all shades of yellows and oranges, it's so nice, those lines at sunset!'

My friend looked at me in a strange way. As my look met hers, a strange feeling occurred inside me. 'Something' was wrong.... Then she said, 'Sylvie, do you really believe what you just said?' By the tone of her voice I knew that something was really wrong.... I answered, 'Err... – yes, of course!' To which she answered, 'Sylvie! Wake up! – there is no such stuff, those lines are pollution'

Then, something was really wrong... within me. As if a whole universe was collapsing.... My classmate found it very special and funny. I didn't – but I kept my feelings to myself.

I have a pro-active nature myself so, that evening, I called a very close friend I had at the time, who also had a very special way of seeing things, and who at the same time held a Ph.D. in physics. He loved my description, and said, 'Only you can think like that! I felt deeply loved just as I was, and then I was able to learn exactly what the white lines were. I became an expert, knowing why they are sometimes thick, sometimes thin, why sometimes they stay longer, sometimes not, what they are made of, and so on.

I must be honest and state that it then took me years to integrate this aspect of my mind that 'saw' white lines as 'pilots wanting to create beauty in the sky'; and up to this day only my closest friends have known of the white-lines story.

Now, I always smile when I see white lines in the sky, and I hope you will too. Remember to watch them when the sun sets, or rises.

III THE MAGIC WAND

The magic-wand event happened in 1998, in London, England, where the Conference and international events of the International Association of Infant Massage were held, with whom I have been working since 1983. For this special occasion, the founder of the Association, Vimala McClure, was present. She is an extraordinary woman, a visionary with exceptional insight whom I truly admire. Because of health difficulties, she mostly walks with a cane. One evening, my dear colleague and friend Mia and I invited Vimala for dinner. We fetched her from her hotel and went to a nearby restaurant.

To my surprise, Vimala did not have her cane. I did not ask why, I just noticed that she was walking slowly, and that she was holding a long white metal stick in her hand. Most of the evening she was holding that stick, as well as all the way back to her hotel. I could observe my mind wondering why she did not have her cane, and what this stick was all about – and also starting to think that perhaps the stick was given to her by a kind of spiritual master, that it had special strength, enough to enable her to walk and be well for a while. I even thought she was using the stick just with Mia and myself and not in front of everyone, trusting us, knowing that we are both open to all possible alternatives in regard to matters of healing. All in all, I even gave the stick the name of 'Magic Wand'.

When we arrived back at her room, she took the magic wand and... opened her hotel room with it! It was simply a long, very long key holder (and I had not at all noticed the small key at the end of it)! I did not say a word and was in a state of shock, again, with my own mind and thought process. Mia and I then simply left – our hotel was about a block from hers, so we walked. It was 11 p.m. I then decided to talk to Mia, whom I deeply trust, starting with: 'Mia, I need to share something that I am quite ashamed of...' – and then I told her the whole story.

She laughed so much, she couldn't breathe in hilarious disbelief. Then I started to laugh out loud as well, and I do not even know why I was laughing, really, as I was rather unhappy with myself.... But laughter is contagious, and we were laughing so loudly that a man opened his flat window to shout at us, 'Girls, shut up! – it's eleven o'clock!'.

Then I got scared, as Mia kept repeating, 'I have to tell Vimala, I have to tell Vimala!' – to which I answered, 'Oh no! Oh no! Please, Mia, don't!' She replied, 'Oh yes! I will tell her!' Only God knows how much trouble I felt I was in, but Mia loves me, that I know! So the day after, we went back to Vimala's room as we had 'serious' International Association matters to discuss, and another of our colleagues, DeAnna, was also in the room with Vimala. So... Mia told the story.

As I witnessed the whole process, I started to relax. There was so much love and so much laughter as they were saying, 'Oh! – if everyone within our Association knew that the International Board IAIM's President thinks that the founder walks around with her magic wand, maybe they wouldn't elect her again!' Yes, that is me....

The story doesn't end there. Three whole months after the event, I received a packet from Vimala. I opened it – there was a letter, and... a 'magic wand'. A beautiful one, in metal, ending with a star, solid and made of recycled metal, that really looked like the wand Vimala had had in London. The letter indicated that the wand was to give me all powers to offer positive guidance for our Association, inspired by wisdom.

The Magic Wand is near my bedroom window, beside a dream catcher that was made especially for me by traditional Native people from British Columbia, to whom I have been teaching the art of infant massage. They have put four beads of different colours on it, telling me that it is because they want my words to go North, South, East, and West.

So be it, with modesty, gratitude, and joy.

PART TWO

THE SONG

THE SONG IN MINOR

No Idea

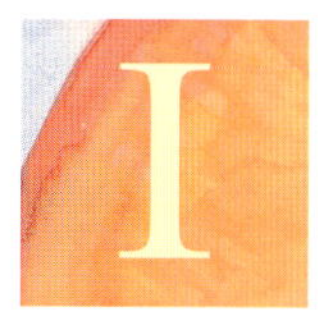
do not know, I do not know how to love and be loved by you.

I am Scared!

ll I need is for you to understand how scared I am.
All it is, is that I am so scared, so scared!

Safe Ice

o! Do not melt the ice around my heart!
My heart finds its home in the ice.
Protected from the sword of the dark knight who once pierced it.
Without the ice, my heart would have been a
spout to let all the blood out of my body.

The Purring Wild Cat

o you really think that I am a wild cat....
And all you want from me is to become a nice playful kitten.
How can I do that if you really believe that I am a wild cat?
You think I am so wild that you want to put me in the wilderness of the dark forest again,
so that monsters can take care of me.
You really think that I am a wild cat
and now you want to put me in a cage
so I will learn to be contained.
You want to trap me!
I will go more wild!

A Mess

P lease accept me with my mess,
for my mess is not me,
just one expression of my blankness,
or something I learned the wrong way.

The Heartbeat

y heart beats, just like yours.
It sometimes goes crazy,
just like yours,
out of fear
or out of pure unknown-ness.

Lost Ground

do not know where the ground is,
I do not know where to put my feet,
it is so dark in the forest,
my feet are scared to
be caught by unknown traps.
My feet are frozen,
my feet lack eyes to find out where
tricky roots are.
Where is the safe ground so that my feet stop fearing holes?

Me: Strong

o you think I am weak?
Really?
You think I am a poor little weak thing?
Just a wimp?
And you wonder how come I still kick, yell, bite?
I want to show you how strong I am!

How Could I know?

ow could I know that I can use words instead of yelling,
How could I know that I can dig a hole in the sand instead of kicking you,
How could I know that I can dance instead of
banging my head on the wall?
How could I know that I can climb trees instead of having you climb walls when you look at me?

What Hands Hide

hen you will first touch me, I may be convinced
that you hide a knife, a rock,
a snake, or a snail in your hands.
This is what hands may hide.
This is what I know hands may hide.
How can I be sure of your hands, how can I open mine to yours ?

The Unknown World

Y our world is unknown to me.
All colours, all sounds,
all smells, all songs,
all words, all gestures,
all walls, all doors, all floors…
all are unknown to me.

Out of the Mouth

hat else do you think I could do other than spitting?
I need to extinguish the fire of the dragons.
How do I even know that fire will not come out of *your* mouth?
And now you do not like my words?
Who do you think you are?
You have better words?
I know no more words than those that were said to me.

The Safe Deep Black Hole

am trapped in a hole, a deep black hole.
It was the safest place for me, you understand?
In the dark forest of all monsters,
in all directions I would go,
I would meet with a monster, and another,
and another.
How did I learn to fight some of them?
My feet and hands are experts in the matter.
But the last one I met was just too big for me.
I did not even try to fight him.
I jumped in a hole too small for the monster,
But now too high to climb out of.
I am trapped in the black hole.
I have no hope, no food, but it is safe.

Absolutely safe.

The Dragons Ate My ‘Yes’

I want to learn to say ‘yes’
but I don’t know you yet.
I have lost my ‘yes’ in the dark forest
of dangerous dragons.
How do I know that you are not a false King
hiding a dragon, how do I know?
Where is the true kind King?
I became a ‘no’.
Where is my ‘yes’?

What Tears Are Really

ears are worthless and dangerous.
They are in the way, blurring our eyes when monsters come to attack you.
They remove your strength to fight the monsters.
I know that well.
Plus, you need to know that dragons
do not like the tears at all.
They are a threat to the awful fire
coming out of their mouths.
So when they see tears,
they really, really, really become wild
and you lose the battle with them.
Tears are worthless, as I well know.
Once they start, they are endless.
And no one is there to help you dry your eyes anyway.

The No

I know nothing about a good 'no'.
Nothing.
I had 'yes, yes, yes' as I was left to myself.
I had 'no, no, no' with constant, constant hurt
associated with it.
I may go wild under your 'no', for I have not learned that 'No' can
be filled with love.
I may well go wild.
Understand how scary it is.
I need, but I don't know your arms yet.

The Missing Piece

nd now you wonder why I steal?
Think twice! Maybe I missed something....
When I needed milk, it was not there,
or not at the proper time.
I WAS JUST HUNGRY!
When I needed a song, there was no song but yelling instead.
I was looking for your song.
When I needed a soft warm hand on my head,
there was nothing but darkness, or a slap, or shaking.
And now it is simply that I am all mixed up,
all mixed up, all mixed up about what to take
or not take.
It is simply that it is easier and more comfortable to take what I need
rather than having to ask for it.

In The Far, Alone

o you want to get close to me....
Can you, can you, can you imagine how scary that is for me?
I was hurt by people close to me.
I have developed strategies to seem close to you, but not to let you in.
And I will use all the strategies I have
to stay where I am to feel safe
'in the far alone'.
I will try to control you, make you believe that I am close and OK,
just to hide my fear.
For if I tell you my fears, I will lose the ground of all my known universes.
It is very scary to visit other planets.

Scary Noises

once heard my own song.
I once heard a big, beautiful Song.

Where is it?
Somewhere in my encapsulated heart and soul?

There are too many noises, scary noises,
unknown noises around me.
They are loud, they make me deaf to my song,
to your song, to all songs.
I became deaf, this is all too scary.

How to quieten the loud, bad noises?
How to hear the songs again?
Where has the song of my heart gone?

Can I get it back?
Noises and deafness are so scary.

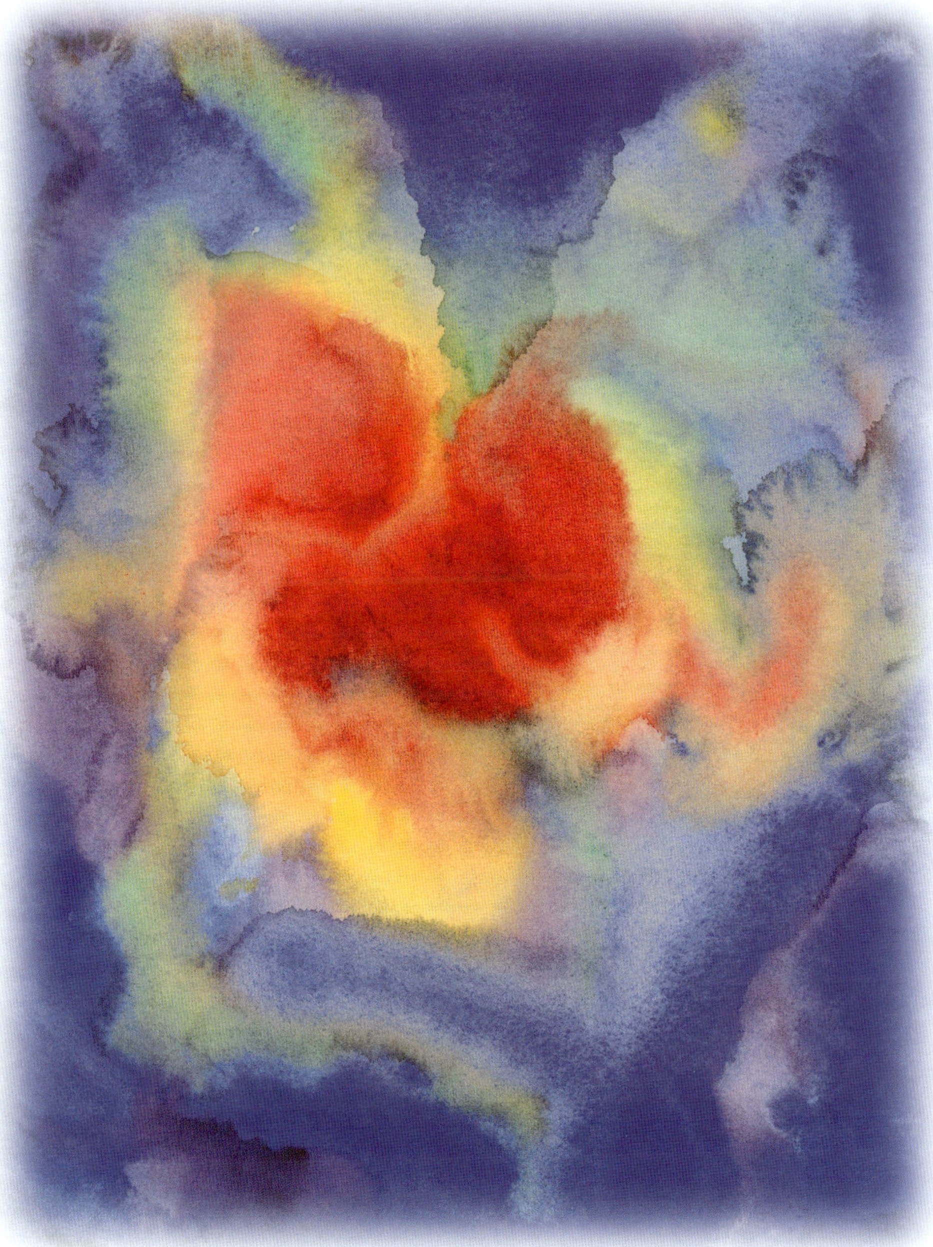

The Far Away Universe

here is it?
I once heard, felt, saw a universe of all colours, all sounds, all dances.

It seemed to be in me. The far away in me.
Where is that far away universe?
It was so warm.

Glimpses, so warm, so light, so soft, so joyful.

I lost my way to it, it seems so far away; I do not know distances.

You sometimes gave me glimpses of that far away universe.
When you gave them to me,
I panicked, confused... scared to lose it again.
I want to cling, cling, cling to that universe.
I want it more, again and again.
I am thirsty for it.

A glimpse? Never enough, never enough.
Not just a short visit!
Always, always living there,
going back in the far away,
I want a way to live there,
never to be far away again.

Locked Longing

I long, oh I long
Deep somewhere in my being,
I long, I long for you, for trusting you.
Do you hear?
I long for you.
But I do not know how to tell you.
I do not know how to let you know.
Let me know that you also long for me,
Let me know that it is worthy to long for you,
Let me know that I do not need to run away
or lock the door.
For I have lost the keys to all the doors.

INTERLUDE

The Mysterious Paradox

f I turn my back to you
If I yell at you
If I cry endlessly
If I act crazy
If I slam the door
If I yell, period –

It may be that I feel
very safe with you,
very loved by you.

B. THE SONG IN MAJOR

You Are My Guide

lease show me,
because you know what you want from me.
But I have no idea how to do it.

Safe Stroking

I am able to purr.
I am.
It is just that I do not know how.
I want to learn to be stroked by you, but
I need to know that you will not hurt me.
I want to learn what is nurturing touch.

The Loving Beat

have heard that my heart can beat faster
because of the blood getting warmer inside me, out of love.
I want this to happen to me.

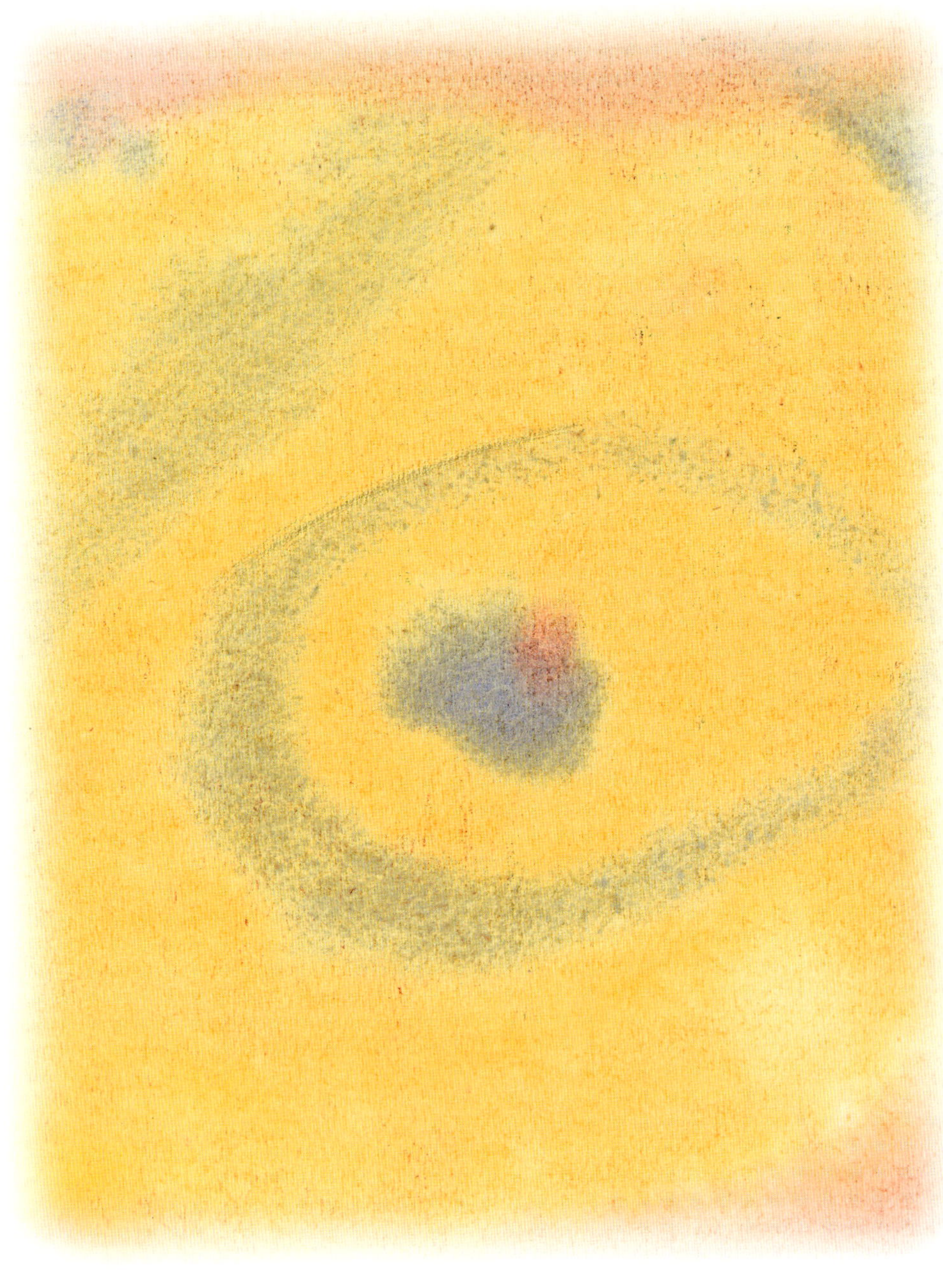

Through Eyes

lease look into my eyes,
through my eyes.
Beneath the doubt,
beneath the fear that you may see,
there is also my longing for your eyes.

Hold My Hand

hen you hold my hand in the dark forest,
my heart gets a light and
my feet get eyes, and I see and
feel the ground.

With Me

ill you cry in the sand with me?
Will you sing with me?
Will you dance with me?
Will you sing for me?
Will you climb in a tree with me
and build a house?

Patience

lease be patient with me,
Touch me slowly,
Tame me.
I wish to open my hands to your hands
instead of closing them.
I wish to play with your hands instead of
you using them against me.
My hands want to learn about you,
about the world,
about what I can create with them.
Aren't they just wonderful?
I can express myself with them.
All of me....

A New World

need guidance for this new world,
for this new home,
for these new smells.

Happy Alone

ou call that a paradox:

'I am happy alone because I have you.'

***

You call that autonomy:

'I am able to do things by myself.'

I laugh! Of course I am able to do things by myself and I have autonomy,
It is because I have *you!*

***

Here is a truth:

'We are all alone, but no one is autonomous.'

Humming the Monsters Away

Please hum to me before you sing
as I cannot recognize music or your song yet.
Hum to me gently so I can start hearing again.
If you sing too loudly, I may think that
it is the sound of monsters in the dark forest.
Then I will be scared and agitated again.
Hum to me, hum me a lullaby,
for lullabies belong between the world of light
and the world of darkness.
You can then help me to create
a safe bridge between the two worlds,
from one to another,
from another to one,
until I understand that there is always light,
Even in darkness.

The Petals

ive me time, give me time,
For I have lost all my strength.
I can't be pushed.
Give me time, give me time to learn.
I will bloom,
I will bloom with the right food for my body,
As I will bloom and grow with the right food for my heart.
My petals will not open if you force them.
They will open only if you provide the right soil,
the right water, the right light.
Only I can decide when I will open my petals,
And then you will have the gift
of my subtle perfume.

The Look that Melts the Ice

y fear of the unknown
pushed my eyes away from you;
please forgive me.
Please teach me that your eyes
looking into my eyes
reveals the warmth of the sunrays,
please help me melt the ice
where my heart is imprisoned,
where my heart cannot beat,
please help me melt the ice so that I can find
the sun in my own heart.

Hold Me – to Peace

Please hold me, hold me strong,
hold me strong
when my body does crazy things.
For my arms and hands and legs
never learned how to rest at peace,
and all I need from you
is that you contain them
so that they learn to behave.
I cannot do that
without you holding me tight
and understanding that it's not *me* who kicked
or pinched, it's not me,
it is my foot that knows nothing else,
it is my hand that knows nothing else.
Show me that they can rest at peace.
Please hold me,
again and again,
again.

My All Directions

I go up, down, up,
Up, up, down, down,
Flat, straight, backwards,
Backwards,
Dance to the side, to the side,
Back, to the other side,
Up, up, up,
Fast, slow, fast, slow,
Slow, slower,
Fiddle, go fast, fast,
Around, around,
Head up, head down,
Down, down.
I swirl, go in lines,
Curved lines, straight lines,
Broken lines, circles, circles,
Oops! A triangle,
Oops! One side goes this way,
My head the other way,
I fall, climb, crawl,
Run, run, run,
Run to you, to you,
Away from you,
Again and never
To you, perhaps.

The Little Lantern

Please give me time, please give me time,
Please be patient.
Deep in my own darkness shines the light,
but nobody ever showed me my way to it.
My little lantern got extinguished
in strong winds.
Please show me a bit of your light
so I can start finding my way.
Please do not make it too bright
as it will hurt my eyes.
Open the curtain slowly,
give the sun the time it needs to rise.
I cannot be noon when it is five in the morning.

Tricking

ou are big to me.
You are threatening to me.
You are wiser than me,
that is how it is supposed to be.
You have all your tricks,
I have all my tricks.
If you try to trick me,
I may want to trick you back.
In my way, I am stronger,
and that is because I am scared
and because my heart is trapped in ice.
Please, act wisely towards me,
but do not trick me.
If you become tricky,
trying to make me do things your way,
trying to make me believe the untrue,
I will just become a better trickster.

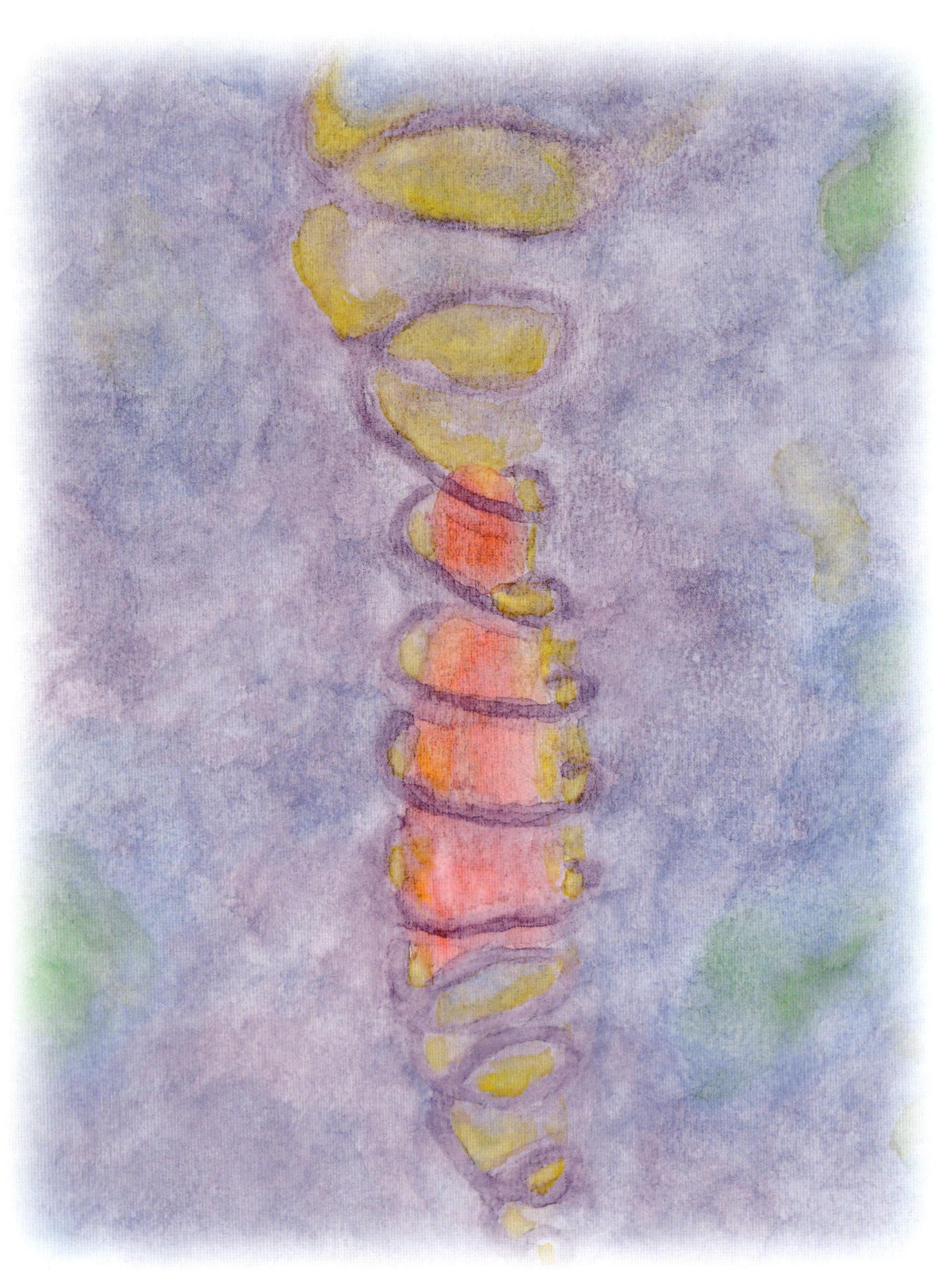

The Cocoon

ou need to know that I am happy alone
Because this is what feels safe for me.
This is what I have learned.
I may look like I do not want
to be with you or others.
This is only because this is what I know.
I have learned to be with myself.
I have wrapped myself in a cocoon.
If you open the cocoon too quickly,
you will only find a mushed-up caterpillar.
Give me time to become
a butterfly.

Again and Again

f you introduce me to the land
of 'looking at me, singing to me,
holding me, tickling me, laughing with me,
stroking my hair',
you may end up doing it for hours and hours,
and hours,
as I do not know these things and
I learn by repetition,
repetition, repetition,
repetition....
Will you, will you, will you?
Please be patient with me
Patient
  Patient
    Patient
      Patient

Eyes, Nose, Ears

y eyes smell, my nose hears, my ears see.
Oops!
Did I mix myself up?

My nose sees, my eyes hear, my ears smell.

Giggles…
Let's try again

My ears hear, my nose sees, my eyes smell.

More giggles…
Almost?

My eyes see, my ears hear, my nose smells –
Right!
NO! … Right AND wrong.
Because the answer is ALL of the above!
The real answer is ALWAYS all of the above.
I PERCEIVE by all means, and then:
As true as all of the above,
which is always true,
I FEEL!

You Doubt Me?

isten.
I smell and I immediately 'see'
what is cooking.

I see a violin
and I 'hear' it.

I hear the sound of a bell
and I 'see' how big it is.

I am one, all one, with all my senses.

If you touch me,
my heart knows you.
It is true, as is all of the above.

As soon as you think that
there is only one answer,
you trick yourself,
and me as well.

The Moon

hat moon, that beautiful moon
that talks to me about
the light of the sun with other tones...

Light of the Moon, of the Sun...

On the other side, what is there?
You tell me it is dark...
I believe it is the whole Universe
on the other side, mysteriously dark.
But a mystery is appealing and holds light as well.

Oh! – an eclipse! How strange,
the moon disappearing under my eyes!
The light becoming dark under my eyes! But look! –
As the moon disappears, more stars appear...
How strange... the darkness brings up
all these little lights to shine!

You and I, maybe we are like the moon.
We appear and disappear.
We are light and dark.
Sometimes, when there is too much light,
my eyes go blind! How strange.
If I put my hand up and create shadow,
then I see again. How strange.
More little stars when the moon disappears.
The shadow gives my eyes
the possibility of seeing something else.

The Moon plays Hide and Seek!
I love to play Hide and Seek with you.

The Sponge with Billions of Holes

es! Yes! Yes!

I am a big sponge with holes, billions of holes,
tunnels, labyrinths, caves, and openings.

I soak in everything. I take in everything.
Everything.

My world is the water of all oceans,
I breathe all waters in and out.

I nourish my whole being from everything
the water surrounding me contains.
I have absolutely no filters,
I am the filter,
so I take in everything, I keep everything.
I was born to trust that
water was all good for me.
Everything of the water flows into me,
circulates through me, shapes me, inflates me.
My whole me.
I am one with all waters.

My Song

n my Song
resonates all Songs
since all Songs are notes
from the Song
of the whole Universe.

Simplicity and Eternity

lease show me who you are
with simplicity.
For this I need, but do not yet know.

Please show me that at times,
time stretches like eternity, an eternity where we can simply talk,
look at each other, laugh.

I have no sense of your time,
the time you call 'hours',
and have no understanding
of how to act upon it.

Please show me slowly. I call for your patience.
If you force me, I may become wild.

If you create the space,
I may learn to be safe, in time.

What you call 'time' is a line for you,
but round for me.
Round, eternal, blended with space,
with no start and no end.

'Wait a minute' is an unknown idea for me,
as well as 'we will be late'.

For eternity stretches in all directions for me,
all directions.

Woven in Gold

he Needle of Life should pierce my heart,
for if it does not, how can I feel part of
the tapestry of the 'All living on Earth'?

The Needle of Life should pierce my heart
and weave its Golden Thread through it.

The Infinite Golden Thread comes from ever and goes to ever.
It is carried by hands and wings which hold the Needle.

Please prepare my heart for life
and help me care for its golden wound.

Between Earth and Sky

stand solid with my magic roots
you call 'feet'.

My magic roots carry magic sap
from the heart of the Earth
to the core of my being.

The sap is so magic, it eternally expands
and grows me fruits and wings.

Then I can fly as high as I can,
blending my own seeds
with the light of the Stars.

Celebration, a Moment

bserve me as I observe life,
For when I observe life I am one with it.

I do not think about what is.
I am WITH the 'what is' .

Indeed, I do not observe life, I *am* life.

I am married with life,
Life that unfolds
with me
through me
in me
in every gesture
in every moment
in every everything.

I am one in the Whole, the Whole in One.

Please observe this ever-eternal moment of celebration.

In the End

o you really know, *really* know where I came from
and where I am going?

Isn't there still a mystery in your quest,
in our quest?

Isn't there still a big uncertainty about
many of the questions I bring with me?

In the end perhaps my quest is
the same as yours;
In the end perhaps all I need is to share
the mystery of who I strive to become,
with you.

In the end, it may not even be
what I become that is important,
but that you and I together accept
that we are mysteriously…
becoming.

PART THREE

The Answer

hild, I will be patient.
Child, I will walk with you.
Together we will venture into the dark forest
and together we will fight the monsters.
Together we will take the dragons by the tail
and we will swing them beyond
the end of the universe.
Together we will choose close-to-good dragons,
pull out coloured ribbons,
attach them around their necks and ride them.
These dragons will become your friends
to help you when you meet the monsters.
If wolves with long teeth appear in front of you,
we will pull out the teeth.
We will tie up snakes in trees,
so that they fight with each other
instead of with you.

In the dark forest,
we will find our way
amongst the dense bushes.

Our dragon friends will help us
to burn the eyes of ogres.

The dark forest will have paths with light.

We will discover springs,
and we will drink fresh water
and will dance with water fairies.

A gentle breeze will caress our skin
and, looking above,
patches of blue sky will peak
through the branches of big trees.

We will see the sun coming out of the thick grey clouds,
and warming rays, shining,
will guide us on our way through the forest.

We will walk for hours,
days, months,
out of time.
Over and over again,
I will take your hand.
You know my hand has only but
warmth and love for you.

If it becomes dark again
and we fall on rocks,
we will have each other to help us get back up.

Again and again, our feet will learn
how to stand and walk around the obstacles.
If we fall in a hole,
we will have each other
and our dragon-friends' long tails
to climb back up.

Gradually, the trees will become less and less,
the forest will feel less dense.

We will reach a field
where wheat dances with the wind,
where flowers of all colours

bathe under sunrays,
offering us multiple shapes,
perfumes and dances.

We will be friends with bees
who will give us honey instead of stinging us.

We will walk and walk
and I will put my arm around your shoulders
and feel the life in your body,
and you will feel my warmth
in a new way.

We will walk and walk
and then we will rest.
We will lie in the field
and we will look at the infinite blue sky,
decorated with white fluffy clouds of all shapes.
In those clouds, sheep, smiling elephants,
sailing boats, and hares will appear.

Across the sky,
we will see air planes drawing their way.
We will laugh together,
basking in our joyful abandon.

The sun will go down.
The sky, the clouds,
the air plane drawings
will become orange, purple,
red, yellow.
You will be quiet.
You will open and close your eyes
as you never did before.

Night will come,
dragon friends will come around us,
protecting us.

They will light a nice fire near us,
to keep us warm.
They will be our guardians
and our light in darkness.
Your head on my shoulder
will make you feel safe.
Waking up to a new day,
we will eat whatever delights come to hand,
blueberries, strawberries, raspberries –
all berries!
Oh! – an apple will be waiting for us,
round and red,
ready to be tasted.

I will look at your face
and laugh at the red and purple around your lips
and on your cheeks.
There will then be sadness and disappointment
expressed on your face,
as you will not understand my laughter.
You will then turn your back to me.

Then, I will cover my own face with berries.
Whilst you turn your head quickly
to see if I am still there,
you will start laughing at me,
and again we will join in laughter.

And here you are!
Your face on my white shirt!
I will start tickling you until tears of laughter
stream out from your eyes.

Your hand in my hand,
we will walk again
until the deep blue of the sea emerges.

What is happening?

I feel your body all stiff, and you scream:
'No, no! The ocean hides sharks!'
Then I will wait,
stand for eternity beside you,
holding your hand with endless patience.
Then from far away,
dolphins, friends of humans,
will swim towards us.
They will offer us their beauty,
they will jump, twirl, and sing for us.
Your hand will leave my hand
and wave to them.
Slowly we will approach the water
and they will invite us to swim with them.
We will hop up on to their backs,
and they will keep us safe from the sharks.
Together with them
we will discover corals of all shapes,
fish of magnificent radiant colours.
We will ride fast,
we will ride slow.
We will waltz and rock, free,
feeling the wind, the sun, the water,
alive.

Before we know it,
it will be time to say goodbye,
and they will give you and me
amazingly beautiful seashells.
We will admire them with awe,
hold them near our hearts
and promise we will cherish them for ever.
The dolphins will tell us
that if we take care to keep our shells safe,
they will grant us the title
of Dolphins on Earth,
active reminders and promoters
of the singing symphony of all living beings.

Walking back towards the forest,
you will fall on your knees again.
Your head will shake a 'No'.
I will take your hand again,
but you will bite it,
you will kick me.

I will try to feel how scared you are
and remind you that you have dragon friends,
waiting for you,
ready to help you go back into the forest.

I will ride on a dragon with you,
holding you very tight
so that your body, legs, and hands are contained
and rest at peace.

Slowly, your body will relax again.

We will pause in the middle of the forest,
and rest.
Suddenly, tears will be rolling down your cheeks
and you will want to stop them.
Feeling ashamed,
you will want to hide them from me.
You will hide your face in your hands.

Your eyes peeking out between your fingers,
you will see tears rolling down my own cheeks.
Gradually, you will remove your hands
and I will open my arms to you.
Hesitating, you will come closer,
finally nestling yourself against my body,
and you will cry again.
Your whole body will cry,
not only your eyes will cry,
and cry, and cry.
For hours, for eternity,

for all the tears of your universe,
I will hold you.

My hand that you learnt to trust
will stroke your head endlessly,
until you calm down
and finally fall asleep.

Waking up with a smile
you will spring up on your legs,
ready to walk again.
You are quick,
I run behind you!
Where are you?
I don't see you any more.
You fell in a hole again!
How can I reach you?
It seems so deep and dark down there,
way down there....
To my astonished surprise,
you will whistle to your dragon friends,
and in a breeze they will be there.
With their long tails,
they will lift you up
and there you will be,
laughing, sparkling.

Your laughter will resonate infinitely,
as if all the bells on earth were singing!

Whilst we walk again together in the forest,
new sounds will be heard by you.
Wind in the branches,
leaves cracking under your steps, bird songs,
a chipmunk happy to have found a chestnut.

You will discover the beautiful hidden creatures
of the forest.

We will point them out to each other.

The deer mother,
so dear to her baby,
the fox with its endless beautiful tail,
a family of green frogs
sleeping on the lily pads of a little pond.

What is this?
An incredible structure of branches.
What is this?
Strangely cut trees all over.
Watch! Watch,
silently, respectfully,
not to disturb.

Hiding behind the tree
we will observe the work of this genius beaver,
admiring his engineering and architect's skills.

A strange happening will catch our attention.
A round white cocoon
from which movement is perceptible.
Beyond time,
we will watch the birth of a butterfly,
opening with strength and courage
its wrinkled wings to the gentle wind
and the warm rays.
You will tell me that
maybe butterflies are flying flowers.

You will also think that trees
produce flying flowers
when a magnificent, proud, shining bird
will fly out of a tree,
radiant with fluffy red feathers.

We will get to climb back on the dragons
and ride fast,
holding our coloured ribbons
as you wish to follow the course of the bird.

We will then reach the end of the forest
and begin to see horses.
You will stop your dragon,
step down, stop smiling,
a glazed look coming over you.
You will sit.

I will try to hold your hand
but you will resist,
protecting yourself with your arms
and pulling your legs close to your chest.
I will talk to you,
you will cover your ears with your hands.

I will try to lift you into my arms
but you will be heavier than a rock.
Then I will sit nearby
and read my favourite book.

For a long moment,
we will just be there.
You will remove your hands from your ears
and shout at me, 'Leave me alone!'

I will continue reading my book.
You will stand up and start running back
towards the forest.
I will lift my head
and assure myself that
your dragon friends are with you.

From very far away in the forest,
I will then hear you
calling my name out loud.

I will track you down
and find you in tears,
your arms reaching to me.
I will hold you,
you will cry in my arms.
Then, I will hum
one of my favourite songs to you.
You will hear me,
you will feel the song
vibrating on my chest,
you will be comforted.

'I don't want to see all the houses.'
I will listen.
'I am scared of the people in the houses.'
I will listen again,
I will hold you again,
I will taste your tears again.

Taking your hand
I will simply say that there is no need
to go into houses right now.
Then you will accept walking again.
Simply, we will walk past houses
of all shapes and colours,
and we will come across
people walking.
We will simply walk,
walk, walk.
Sometimes you will leave my hand,
sometimes you will hold it tight.

Again I will hum my favourite song to you,
and you will then have learnt it
and will hum it with me.
People will smile, seeing us both walking and humming,
even if we are new in their village.
We will sit on a bench

near the little river
that runs through the village,
giving it light, freshness, and life.
We will see the sunset
reflecting on the water,
its still, warming rays
giving the impression that the whole village
has been painted in pink by an artist.
The pink hour.
Clouds and air plane drawings
make no exception.
Pink.

Softly,
out of nowhere and from everywhere
you will start singing.
You will sing me a song.
Your Song.

Strangely, it will be easy for me
to sing it with you,
as if I had heard it before.

I will sing it with you,
endlessly.

You know my song.
I know your song.

You will look into my eyes.
I will look into your eyes.

Deeply, at last,
I will know that you know
that I see you.
I will know that you see me.

I see you
I hear you
I feel you
I sing with you.

How lucky am I,
to have learnt your song.

You will turn your head towards the little village,
you will point out the blue house.
'That is my favourite',
will be your words.

We will walk towards the house
and I will let you knock on the door
all by yourself.

For now, child,
you meet with your destiny
and share your songs
with the world.

Afterword: from the child

I am most grateful that you took the time to read about me. If you still need to foster your learning about me, keep it simple. There are simple mysteries about me. To help you, consult the book *The Little Prince,* by Antoine de Saint-Exupéry. Discover the Little Prince's link with the Rose, and his story with the Fox. You may then feel, deep in your heart, that part of the mystery is all about taming, is all about love, is all about being unique to someone.

The Child

APPENDIX

INSPIRING READINGS

It would greatly exceed the number of pages that I want for this book if I were to list all the books that have contributed in one way or another to giving birth to *The Song of the Child.*

I wish indeed to honour all authors who have taken time in their lives to explore the mystery of our human condition, to try to give it meaning and inspiration.

I will list just a few of them here – the ones that obviously live most strongly in my own soul – together with some simple reasons why. I hope that this may perhaps help readers on their own particular quests.

Elaine N. Aron (1999) The Highly Sensitive Person, Element/Harper Collins, London, 251 pp
A book that helps any adult to understand how high sensitivity can hinder an extraordinary potential from being fully expressed. Helps anyone to understand how all young children may experience the world and people around them, and the repercussions for future adult life. Written with tremendous knowledge and insight.

Rahima Baldwin (1989) You Are Your Child's First Teacher, Celestial Arts, Berkeley, California, 376pp
This book, inspired in part by Steiner educational principles and practice, is very comprehensive, guiding parents toward a conscious and knowledge-based approach to raising children. Combines deep insight with day-to-day practical aspects of child-rearing.

John Bowlby (1988) A Secure Base: The Making and Breaking of Affectional Bonds, Routledge, London, 180pp
This is a collection of lectures given by the great John Bowlby, who for the first time brought to human consciousness the crucial importance of a secure, loving, early-year attachment, or bond, between the baby child and the caring adult. His work has been picked up and deepened by thousands of therapists in all fields, and reading any book by Bowlby wakes us up to the unquestionable importance of the loving and empathic care of babies and young children.

Diana Carey and Judy Large (1982) Festivals, Family and Food, Hawthorn Press, Stroud, 224pp
A book that brings us back to the simple yet essential joy of celebrating and anticipating the seasons – and, indeed, any special occasion for celebration. It provides a myriad of practical and inspiring ideas to put into action the kinds of meaningful activities that we all surely wish to share with our children.

Dotty Coplen (1995) Parenting for a Healthy Future, Hawthorn Press, Stroud, 131pp
A simple, to-the-point yet profound parenting book, based on Steiner educational principles. An excellent start for those who want to approach Steiner education with simplicity and clarity.

Richard House (2003) Therapy beyond Modernity: Deconstructing and Transcending Profession-centred Therapy, Karnac Books, London, 330pp
A book that any therapist seriously willing completely to 'rethink' the nature, purpose, motivations, and aims of therapy should read. Thought-provoking and extremely well documented, it plants seeds for 'imagining' other ways of considering human development and therapeutic approaches.

Daniel A. Hughes (1998) Building the Bonds of Attachment: Awakening Love in Deeply Troubled Children, Jason Aronson Inc., Northvale, NJ, 312pp
A book that is profoundly helpful for any therapist or social worker whose mission is to help children with challenging biographies, and their caring adults, find a path toward balance and the healing of painful wounds. Combines a beautifully written fictional story of a little girl with an innovative therapeutic approach which illustrates modern knowledge of attachment theories and genuinely deep empathy for children.

Freya Jaffke (1991) Work and Play in Early Childhood, Anthroposophic Press, Hudson, New York, 79pp (and Floris Books, Edinburgh, 1996)
A book that educates any adult caring for young children about the true nature and the crucial importance of play for young children. Is enlightening about the fundamental notions of rhythm, repetition, and imitation as pillars for early learning.

Marshall H. Klaus and Phyllis H. Klaus (1998) Your Amazing Newborn, Perseus Books, Cambridge, Mass., 114pp
A unique book in raising awareness about the extraordinary capabilities and uniqueness of new-born babies. It has magnificent photographs as well as documented studies and research findings revealing amazing discoveries about babies.

Martin Large (2003) Set Free Childhood: Parents' Survival Guide to Coping with Computers and TV, Hawthorn Press, Stroud, 240pp
Provocative, yes. Eye opening, yes. A book that dares to address the influence of television on children, at all levels of their development – cognitive, emotional, social, and so on. We often conveniently want to avoid even thinking about what is revealed in this challenging book. The good news is that the book also offers practical advice for moving on... and for changing entrenched habits – for the sake of our children.

Bernard Lievegoed (1997) Phases of Childhood: Growing in Body, Soul and Spirit, Anthroposophic Press, Hudson, NY, 208pp
A book that initiates all readers to the knowledge about childhood development from birth to 21 years of age, based on Rudolf Steiner's indications. We learn how soul and body correlate one with the other, and how this understanding becomes a reliable guide to educating and interacting with children.

Vimala McClure (1999) The Path of Parenting: Twelve Principles to Guide Your Journey, New World Library, Novato, California, 257pp
A book that breathes in and out, one that guides us on the journey of the 'out of time and space' sensibility that is so needed on the parenting path. Easy, and at the same time practical and poetic, yet also profound, encompassing values that I consider perennial in the raising of children.

Rudolf Meyer (1997) The Wisdom of Fairy Tales, Floris Books, Edinburgh, 267pp
A very valuable book to help us understand the inner wisdom of fairy tales, their meaning, and how they can have a profoundly positive influence on the developing child. All characters in fairy tales being elements of our human nature, it is really interesting to discover how their archetypal aspects, and the way in which they evolve in fairy tales, can become 'educators' of our deep self.

Lynne Murray and Liz Andrews (2000) The Social Baby, The Children's Project Ltd., London, 176pp
A truly up-to-date research-based book about the grandeur and uniqueness of babies, who indeed have a complex yet fabulous psychological life right from birth. Any adult in contact with babies will gain useful information that will enhance their understanding and communication skills with babies. The whole book induces profound reverence and respect for babies.

Karen Reivich and Andrew Shaffé (2003) The Resilience Factor, Broadway Books, New York, 342pp
A book that gives hope to adults who experienced a challenging childhood, or to those working with children who exhibit challenging behaviour. Very well thought out, an illuminating contribution to discovering the mystery of resilience.

Antoine de Saint-Exupéry (2003) The Little Prince (60th anniversary edn), Harcourt Children's Books, 96pp
This book goes beyond words. It penetrates with depth, profundity, and inspiration the true nature of the child. *The Little Prince* is an indispensable world-renowned classic, taking us on a journey of wisdom for all times and places. It helps us to regain the lost poetry of childhood, to its very foundations.

Eugene Schwartz (1999) The Millennium Child: Transforming Education in the Twenty First Century, Steiner Books, San Francisco, 320pp
A true inspiration for teachers, educators, parents, and child psychologists, which addresses the highly prescient issue of 'children as an endangered species'. Helps us to look at our mistakes in tandem with a thoughtful analysis of the effect that educational errors have had on children. Brings a totally new paradigm of childhood development and related approaches, inspired by Steiner education.

Betty Staley (1988) Between Form and Freedom: Guiding Teenagers through the Dangerous Years, Hawthorn Press, Stroud, 280pp
A very inspiring book to guide all adults on their journey with teenagers.

Rudolf Steiner (2004) The Spiritual Ground of Education, Steiner Books, 152pp
This book will give any reader food for thought... as it brings the spiritual knowledge of the child, as studied by Rudolf Steiner, to light. The reader will discover a totally new world and will start to journey in usually unknown waters as far as knowledge about human beings goes. Prepare yourself!

Margot Sunderland (2000) Using Story Telling as a Therapeutic Tool with Children, Winslow Press, Oxford, 96pp
A very accessible book suggesting processes and resources for supporting adults who wish to help children experiencing inner challenges to find a way to resolution. We also gain exact knowledge of the philosophy and psychology behind the use of story-telling as a therapeutic tool.

*****

Finally, I invite readers to enter the world of traditional fairy tales. From any country, any culture, any edition, any language, any age, any year....

About the Author

Sylvie Hétu is the mother of three children, Étienne (b. 1983), Jean-Michel (1986), and Joannie (1990).

Trained as a pre-school and elementary teacher at Montreal University, after several years of working in day-care and schools, her contribution to life has been focussed on the well-being of children at many levels, mainly through adult education. Besides being a dedicated mother, she has been active in the International Association of Infant Massage (www.iaim.net) since 1983, first as an instructor teaching parents the art of nurturing touch; then as a trainer, training instructors in many countries around the world; and finally as the International Board President for 12 years. Sylvie continues to be active within the IAIM International Education Committee. She is also a trained Steiner (Waldorf) teacher (1998), and since then has led Steiner-inspired workshops for, and given talks to, parents and educators in various countries. Together with her Swedish colleague Mia Elmsäter, in 2000 she co-founded the Massage in Schools Programme (www.massageinschools.com), which is now growing rapidly across the globe. She has recently created the 'Working Together' programme, inspiring people to develop comprehensive approaches and progressive attitudes toward working together within associations and organizations at both human and structural levels.

Sylvie is in the process of creating 'EnaPlay', a programme that will explore and foster comprehension of the deep nature of play for children, and the crucial importance needed to be given to the matter for children's true unfolding in life.

Finally, with Richard House she is the co-founder of Ur Publications (www.urpublications.com), and has many books in gestation in the broad fields of education, human and organizational relations, and consciousness evolution.

Paintings

The author would like to express her gratitude to the following people for their artistic (water colour) contributions.

- *I Am Scared*
- *Out of the Mouth*
- *You Are My Guide*

Jean-Michel Hétu-Gossard

- *The Heartbeat*
- *Safe Stroking*
- *Through Eyes*

Étienne Hétu-Gossard

- *Patience*
- *Hold Me – to Peace*
- *Tricking*

Joannie Hétu-Gossard

- *The Little Lantern*

Adèle P. Frenette

- *Simplicity and Eternity*

Sylvie Pasquin

Cover page by the author (crayons)

All other water colour paintings by the author

MISSION STATEMENT

Ur Publications wishes to bring to a wide readership, pioneering thinking at the leading-edge of evolving ideas within education, individual and social development, psychology and related fields – endeavouring to foster insight and creative impulses in these domains of human culture.

OUR UNDERTAKING

In accordance with social philosopher Rudolf Steiner's indications on the social question and the 'Three-fold Social Order' – in which human activities are arranged into three distinct, self-managed, and relatively autonomous spheres, viz. the cultural, the political, and the economic – Ur Publications guarantees to use a substantial proportion of its surplus to support cultural sphere activities, such as arts and education, according to associative economics principles.[1]

[1] For more information about associative economics, visit www.ae-institute.com

Ur Publications wishes to hear about you

Ur Publications' founders wish to stay close to their readers, and we invite direct feedback on our published books. We would appreciate it if you would fill out the following form and return it to Ur Publications. Alternatively, you can share your comments directly on our website, at www.urpublications.com

1.Where did you first hear about, find, or buy *The Song of the Child?*

2. What are your impressions of the book?

3. In the light of Ur Publications' Mission Statement (see page 160), what specific subjects or themes would you welcome in our future publications?

Please send this form with your comments to:

Ur Publications
3232, av. Lacombe
Montréal, Québec
H3T 1L7 Canada

Tel: 514.342.3772
Fax: 514.342.8422
or write to us directly at:
info@urpublications.com